Extreme Skateboarding Moves

By Jeri Freimuth

Consultant:
T. Eric Monroe
United Skateboarding Association

CAPSTONE
HIGH-INTEREST
BOOKS

an imprint of Capstone Press
Mankato, Minnesota

Capstone High-Interest Books are published by Capstone Press
151 Good Counsel Drive, P.O. Box 669, Mankato, Minnesota 56002
http://www.capstone-press.com

Library of Congress Cataloging-in-Publication Data
Freimuth, Jeri.
    Extreme skateboarding moves/by Jeri Freimuth.
    p.cm.—(Behind the moves)
    Includes bibliographical references (p. 31) and index. 32p
    ISBN 0-7368-0783-7
        1. Skateboarding—Juvenile literature. [1. Skateboarding. 2. Extreme sports.]
I. Title. II. Series.
GV859.8. F74 2001
796.22—dc21   00-009842

Summary: Discusses the sport of extreme skateboarding, including the moves
involved in the sport.

Editorial Credits
Angela Kaelberer, editor; Karen Risch, product planning editor; Kia Bielke,
    cover designer and illustrator; Katy Kudela, photo researcher

Photo Credits
Angela Liu, 7, 15 (top)
Brian Appio, 20
David Madison/Bruce Coleman Inc., 4 (inset)
Gregg Andersen, 4, 12, 14, 17
Houston Wood Deaton/Graphicstock, 15 (bottom), 16
Marcelo Moreno/Mercury Press, cover
Mark Turner, 24
Patrick Batchelder, 12 (inset), 21, 22, 24 (inset)
SportsChrome-USA/Michael Zito, 9, 10, 18 (inset); Rob Tringali, Jr., 18, 27, 28

1 2 3 4 5 6 06 05 04 03 02 01

Table of Contents

The ollie is the basic skateboarding trick.

Learn about:

- Ollies
- Types of skateboarding
- Equipment

4

Extreme Skateboarding

Skateboarder Alan Gelfand grew up in Florida in the late 1970s. His friends called him "Ollie." In 1978, Gelfand invented a new skateboarding move.

Gelfand liked to slide his board along the top edge or lip of a skateboard ramp. He practiced this lip slide often. He learned to lift the skateboard into the air during the lip slide. He stepped down hard on the back of his board. This made the board's front or nose pop up. Gelfand's friends called his trick the "Ollie pop."

Gelfand practiced his trick. He learned to pop his board 2 feet (.6 meter) off the ramp. Other skateboarders learned to do the trick. They shortened the trick's name to the ollie. Almost all of today's extreme skateboarding moves begin with the ollie.

The First Skateboards

No one knows who invented the skateboard. Some people say the first skateboard was made around 1900. It might have been a scooter with the handle broken off. It also might have been a board with roller skate wheels nailed to the bottom.

Few people knew about skateboarding until the 1950s. At that time, surfers in California helped make skateboarding popular. The surfers built their own wooden skateboards to practice surfing on land.

By 1959, people could buy skateboards in stores. These skateboards had wooden boards called decks. The decks were attached to four metal wheels.

Improved Skateboards

In the 1960s, skateboard companies replaced skateboards' metal wheels with baked clay wheels. These wheels rolled faster than the metal wheels did.

By the 1970s, skateboard companies found other ways to improve skateboards. They replaced the clay wheels with urethane wheels. These hard plastic wheels rolled easier over cement than metal or clay wheels did. Companies also used metal axles called trucks to attach the wheels to the deck. The trucks help the wheels turn easier. Skateboards have two trucks. Each truck holds two wheels.

Skateboard companies also added a kicktail to the board's rear. This piece of wood curves up from the deck. Skateboarders rest their back foot against the kicktail as they skate. They also use the kicktail to lift the board's nose during tricks.

Skateboards have two trucks.

Types of Skateboarding

The three main types of skateboarding are streetstyle, freestyle, and ramp. Many skateboarders practice more than one type of skateboarding.

Streetstyle skateboarders skate on streets and outdoor obstacles such as curbs, railings, and stairs. Freestyle skateboarders perform tricks on flat surfaces such as parking lots and basketball courts.

Ramp skateboarders can skate on either miniature or vertical ramps. Skaters call these ramps "mini ramps" and "vert ramps."

Mini-ramp skateboarders perform tricks on wooden courses. These courses have small ramps placed at different levels. These ramps are usually between 3 and 6 feet (.9 and 1.8 meters) high.

Vert-ramp skateboarders skate on ramps with straight, vertical walls. Many of these ramps are half-pipe ramps. These ramps have two curved walls connected by a flat area. The curved areas are called transitions. Most half-pipe ramps are between 8 and 12 feet (2.4 and 3.7 meters) high.

Skateboarders skate up and down the half-pipe ramp's curved walls. They perform tricks in the air at the top of the walls. Most vert ramps have a metal railing at the top. This railing is called a coping. Skateboarders often perform tricks on the coping.

Skateboarders skate on vert ramps.

Ramp skateboarders use wide boards.

Types of Skateboards

Skateboarders use different skateboards for each type of skateboarding. The skateboard's size and features are designed to improve skateboarding performance.

Street skateboarders use boards that are about 7.5 inches (19 centimeters) wide. These boards have small, soft wheels that grip the skating surface.

Ramp skateboarders use boards that are about 8 inches (20 centimeters) wide. The wider boards are more stable than the narrower street boards. They also have harder, larger wheels. These wheels roll faster than street skateboard wheels.

Freestyle skateboards are about 5.5 to 6.5 inches (14 to 17 centimeters) wide. They have small, hard wheels. These skateboards are designed for the quick, sharp moves of freestyle skateboarding.

Most skateboarders use grip tape on a board's deck. This adhesive tape keeps skateboarders' feet from slipping as they skate.

A 180 ollie includes a half rotation.

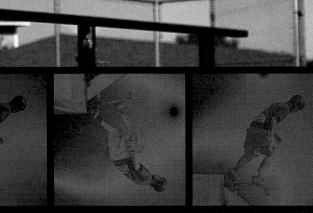

Learn about:

- **Ollies and nollies**
- **Slides and grinds**
- **Kickflips**

Chapter Two

Street Moves

Most skateboarding tricks begin with an ollie. Skateboarders use the ollie to get their boards off the ground without using their hands.

Skateboarders begin an ollie by skating forward. They put one foot on the board's kicktail and push down hard. This motion makes the board's nose pop up. The forward motion carries the board into the air. Skateboarders stay on their boards as they glide through the air. They land with both feet on the board.

Skateboarders perform other forms of the ollie. Skateboarders sometimes rotate their bodies as they perform an ollie. They make a complete rotation during a 360 ollie. They also can do a half rotation. This trick is called a 180 ollie.

Skateboarders also push down on the board's nose as they do an ollie. This trick is called a nollie.

Nose grinds are performed on ledges.

Slides and Grinds

Skateboarders perform slides and grinds on curbs, handrails, and ramp edges. A skateboarder moves the skateboard's wheels across an obstacle to perform a slide. A skateboarder moves the trucks across an obstacle to perform a grind.

Skateboarders begin a slide or grind by doing an ollie to hop onto the obstacle. They slide or grind across the obstacle. They then jump down and land on the board.

Skateboarders perform many types of slides and grinds. To perform board slides, skateboarders slide the board's middle across the obstacle. Skateboarders perform tail

slides by sliding the board across the object on its tail. They perform nose grinds by leaning toward the board's nose and grinding across the front truck. A 5-0 grind is a grind across the back skateboard truck. A 50-50 grind is a grind across both trucks.

Tail slide

A 50-50 grind is a grind across both trucks.

15

Kickflips

Skateboarders often perform kickflips on the street rather than on obstacles. Skateboarders can perform some kickflips while the board is standing still.

Skateboarders often do kickflips on streets.

The board spins in a circle during a 360 flip.

Skateboarders begin a kickflip by doing an ollie to pop the board into the air. They then flip the board by kicking their front foot out and away from their body. The board must make a full turn and land on its wheels. The skateboarder then lands on top of the board.

Skateboarders perform different types of kickflips. Some skateboarders perform 360 flips. During this trick, the skateboard spins in a complete circle before landing.

Skateboarders combine grabs with spins.

Learn about:

Spins and grabs

Handplants and inverts

Flips

Chapter Three

Ramp Tricks

Skateboarders perform some street tricks such as slides and grinds on ramp copings. Skateboarders also use ramps to perform tricks in the air. Skateboarders call these tricks aerials or airs.

Spins and Grabs

Skateboarders use half-pipes to perform spins in the air. A full spin is called a 360. A half spin is called a 180. Some skaters perform 540s or 720s. These skaters spin one-and-one-half or two times in the air. They remain on the board as they spin.

Skateboarders sometimes perform grabs along with spins. They grab the board as they spin through the air. Skateboarders grab the board's nose during a nose grab. They grab the board's kicktail during a tail grab.

Rodeo flips are similar to inverts.

Handplants and Inverts

Skateboarders also perform handplants in half-pipes. An invert is the basic handplant move. This trick looks like a one-handed handstand.

To perform an invert, skateboarders skate quickly up the ramp. Skateboarders hold the board with one hand and place the other on the coping. They balance the board on their feet as they kick their feet into the air. They then turn around toward the ramp. They swing back onto the ramp and skate down.

Flips

A flip is like an invert without the handplant. Skateboarders perform different types of flips.

To perform a rodeo flip, skateboarders skate to the top of the ramp. They flip their bodies around as they grab the board. A handstand flip begins with a one-handed handstand. Skateboarders flip the board around with the other hand while kicking their legs in the air.

An invert is the basic handplant move.

Extreme Skateboarding Slang

bail—to jump off the skateboard before a crash

carve—to perform long, wide turns

cruising—skateboarding without tricks

fakie—to perform a trick backward or opposite of the usual position

goofy-foot position—a skateboarding position where the right foot is in front; regular skateboarding position is left foot in front

hang-up—to catch the trucks on an obstacle

rail—a skateboard's edge

shredding—hard, fast skateboarding

slam—an uncontrolled crash

vert—the vertical wall of a half-pipe ramp; also can mean the half-pipe ramp itself

Skateboard parks are safe places to skate.

Learn about:

■ **Safe skateboarding places**

■ **Safety equipment**

■ **Bailing**

Chapter Four

Safety

Safety has been a problem for skateboarders since the sport's beginning. In the 1960s and 1970s, many cities banned skateboards because too many skateboarders were getting hurt. The sport almost disappeared.

Today, skateboarders and skateboard companies have learned ways to make the sport safer. Skateboarders help build parks where they can skate safely. Skateboard companies make equipment that helps protect skateboarders from injuries.

Safe Skateboarding Places

Some cities have banned street skateboarding. Skateboarders who can ride in their cities' streets must be careful of traffic and people. They must obey skating laws. They also must be careful not to harm other people's property.

Skateboarders can find safer places to skate than streets. Many skateboarders live in cities and towns that have skateboard parks. Other skateboarders skate in empty parking lots.

Safety Equipment

Safe skateboarders always wear helmets and pads. Knee pads and elbow pads protect skateboarders during crashes. Many knee pads are covered with plastic plates. Skateboarders can slide on these plates during a fall.

Many skateboarders also wear wrist guards. Skateboarders often try to catch themselves with their hands as they fall. These skateboarders may break their wrists. Wrist guards have metal or plastic plates.

These plates hold skateboarders' wrists stiff as they fall. This support can prevent the wrist bones from breaking.

Skateboarders should always wear athletic shoes that cover the feet. Shoes protect skateboarders' feet from scrapes and cuts.

Knee and elbow pads protect skateboarders.

Skateboarders kick their boards away as they bail.

Bailing

Skateboarders bail when they know they cannot complete a trick. Skateboarders try to kick their boards away when they bail. Falling on a board can be dangerous.

Safe skateboarders practice bailing on a soft surface such as grass. Knowing how and when to bail can help keep skateboarders safe.

Staying Safe

Most skateboarding tricks are dangerous. Skateboarders need to learn basic skateboarding moves before trying more difficult tricks.

Skateboarders who practice their tricks and follow safety rules are less likely to be hurt. These skateboarders are able to safely enjoy their sport.

Words to Know

aerial (AIR-ee-uhl)—a trick performed in the air

axle (AK-suhl)—a rod in the center of the wheel; the wheel turns around the axle.

freestyle (FREE-stile)—a type of skateboarding performed on level ground

obstacle (OB-stuh-kuhl)—an object that stands in a skateboarder's way; skateboarders perform tricks on obstacles such as curbs and stair railings.

streetstyle (STREET-stile)—a type of skateboarding performed on obstacles found on city streets

transition (tran-ZISH-uhn)—the curve of a ramp between the flat area and the walls

truck (TRUHK)—the metal axle that attaches the wheels to the deck

urethane (YUR-uh-thayn)—a type of hard plastic; skateboard wheels are made of urethane.

To Learn More

Gutman, Bill. *Skateboarding: To the Extreme!*
   New York: T. Doherty Associates, 1997.

Powell, Ben L. *Extreme Sports Skateboarding.*
   Hauppauge, N.Y.: Barron's, 1999.

Ryan, Pat. *Extreme Skateboarding.* Extreme Sports.
   Mankato, Minn.: Capstone High-Interest Books,
   1998.

Useful Addresses

Transworld Skateboarding Magazine
353 Airport Road
Occanside, CA 92054

United Skateboarding Association
P.O. Box 986
New Brunswick, NJ 08903

Vancouver Indoor Skate Park Coalition
801 West 22nd Avenue
Vancouver, BC V5Z 1Z8
Canada

Internet Sites

Skateboarding.com
www.skateboarding.com

Skateboarding in Canada
http://home.earthlink.net/~jay540/index.html

Skatepark.org
www.skatepark.org

United Skateboarding Association
www.unitedskate.com

Index